Paul, Aileen
    Kids cooking without a stove: a
cookbook for young children. Illus. by
Carol Inouye. Doubleday 1975
    63p illus

Easy-to-follow recipes for desserts,
~~~s, salads, sandwiches, snacks, and
~~~les that require no cooking.

~~~ Cookery I;Title

(137)

PAUKCWA

Kids Cooking Without a Stove

Kids Cooking Without a Stove

A Cookbook for Young Children

by Aileen Paul

Illustrated by Carol Inouye

Doubleday & Company, Inc.,
Garden City, New York

To my grandmother, Jessie Deulen Samuelson,
who shared her pleasure in cooking with me.

Other Books by Aileen Paul
Kids Cooking
Candies, Cookies, and Cakes
Kids Cooking Complete Meals
Kids Gardening
Kids Camping

Library of Congress Cataloging in Publication Data

Paul, Aileen.
    Kids cooking without a stove: a cookbook for young
children.

    SUMMARY: Easy-to-follow recipes for desserts, drinks,
salads, sandwiches, snacks, and candies that require no
cooking.
    1. Cookery—Juvenile literature.   [1. Cookery]
I. Inouye, Carol, ill.   II. Title.
TX652.P383 1975   641.5′622
ISBN 0-385-03140-8 Trade
    0-385-03172-6 Prebound
Library of Congress Catalog Card Number 74-3553

Contents

Salads

Sandwiches

Snacks and Candies

Introduction

A group of young but dedicated enthusiasts attended my Saturday Cooking Classes for Children recently. These small boys and girls were four, five and six years old.

These recipes were written especially for them, and none requires the use of a stove by the children. I hope that this book will make it easier for other young children and their parents, older friends, or teachers to enjoy preparing simple but appetizing food.

To Adults

Cooking with small children can be a happy co-operative adventure. Most of the decision making, however, should be in your hands—choosing the right recipe, planning a trip to the grocery store, deciding when the cooking should be done.

It is important to locate a convenient spot in the kitchen for working and to help place supplies and equipment together. A stool may be needed to bring the young child to the correct height at the kitchen counter or table. A small child often likes to kneel on a regular chair which makes him or her high enough for easy working. Being at the right height—so that you reach down instead of up—is important in cooking.

And find a comfortable chair for yourself at the table. There'll be questions to answer and help to be given. Children at this age seldom resent help; but once they're shown how to hold the spoon or use the vegetable peeler, for example, please let them carry on by themselves.

Children remember their first cooking experiences for a long time, and what a joy it is to share them.

To Children

Cooking means getting food ready to eat. You can do that without using the stove. When you are older, say eight or more, you can begin to use the stove with adult help.

The recipes in this book have been used by children your age in my cooking classes. They can be done in thirty minutes to an hour.

Follow the steps and rules on the next pages, and, most of all, have a good time!

Steps to Be Taken

Ask one of your parents, or an older person, to read the recipe to you. Look at the pictures carefully.

You and a grownup should place everything you need together.

If you are using the kitchen table, perhaps it should be covered with a plastic tablecloth.

Keep a damp sponge handy to wipe spills.

Place the garbage pail nearby for easy cleanup.

Rules to Follow

1. Use a table knife for all cutting.
2. Work on a wooden cutting board when cutting. Counter and table tops scratch easily.
3. Do not use any electrical appliances like mixers and blenders.
4. Follow directions exactly.
5. Use the kitchen tools that are suggested.

Things to Use (Equipment)

1-cup, 2-cup, 4-cup measuring cups
nested measuring cups
regular cup
measuring spoons
regular tablespoon
table fork
table knife
mixing spoon
mixing bowls
can opener

egg beater
grater
ice-cream scoop
ice-cube tray
quart jar with lid
rubber spatula
strainer
transparent plastic wrap and wax paper
vegetable peeler
wooden cutting board

Apple Pudding

Here's what you need:

1 cup leftover cooked rice   1-cup measuring cup
1 cup applesauce   measuring spoons
1 teaspoon ground cinnamon   regular tablespoon
1 cup whipped cream (page 22)   4 dessert dishes
medium-size mixing bowl

LET A GROWNUP OPEN THE APPLESAUCE FOR YOU

Here's what you do:

1. Pour cooked rice into mixing bowl.
2. Spoon applesauce into the 1-cup measuring cup up to top line. Add
    to rice.

3. Dip 1-teaspoon measuring spoon into can or jar of cinnamon. Sprinkle over bowl.
4. Mix with ordinary tablespoon.
5. Stir whipped cream gently into rice-applesauce mixture.
6. Spoon into dishes.
7. If you like, you may add a spoonful of whipped cream on top for decoration.

Makes 4 servings

Apricot Banana Cup

Here's what you need:

1 large can (1 pound) apricot
   halves
2 ripe medium bananas
1 pint lemon sherbet
can opener
mixing bowl

table knife
table fork
regular tablespoon
ice-cream scoop
4 to 6 sherbet dishes

ASK AN ADULT TO OPEN CAN AND THROW AWAY TOP

Here's what you do:

1. Empty apricots into bowl with about half of the juice.
2. Peel and slice bananas with table knife. Add to apricots.

3. Mix gently with fork.
4. Spoon into dishes with room left for sherbet.
5. Top each serving with small scoop of lemon sherbet. (Use ice-cream scoop or metal mixing spoon.)

Makes 4 to 6 servings

Cantaloupe Boat

Here's what you need:

1 cantaloupe
1 pint ice cream (vanilla or any
   fruit flavor)
table knife

small spoon
2 medium-size plates
ice-cream scoop

**LET AN ADULT CUT CANTALOUPE IN HALF IF YOUR HANDS ARE
NOT STRONG ENOUGH**

Here's what you do:

1. Take seeds out of cantaloupe with spoon.
2. Place each cantaloupe half on plate.
3. Scoop ice cream. Fill halves of cantaloupe with it.

1 medium cantaloupe serves 2 people

Chocolate Vanilla Parfait

Here's what you need:

1¾ cups milk
1 package instant vanilla pudding
1 can or jar of chocolate syrup
4-cup measuring cup or small
    bowl

egg beater
rubber spatula
4 parfait or sherbet glasses

Here's what you do:

1. Pour milk into 4-cup measuring cup up to 1¾ cup line.
2. Empty package of vanilla pudding into milk.
3. Beat with egg beater until it begins to thicken. Stop and push pudding down from sides of cup with spatula.
5. Beat a few seconds more.
6. Spoon small amount of pudding into each parfait glass. Slowly add thin layer of chocolate syrup. Add more pudding. End with chocolate syrup.

                                                 Makes 4 servings

English Trifle

Here's what you need:

6 thick slices poundcake

1 small jar raspberry jam

18 to 24 ladyfingers

1 to 1½ cups orange juice

1 cup whipped cream (page 22)

table knife

wooden cutting board

shallow serving dish or platter

1-cup measuring cup

Here's what you do:

1. Slice cake with table knife on wooden board.
2. Place slices in shallow serving dish or platter.
3. Spread jam on cake.
4. Dip ladyfingers into orange juice. Place on top of cake. Use enough to cover cake.
5. Spread whipped cream over ladyfingers with table knife. Place in refrigerator to chill.

Makes 6 to 8 servings

Note: Ladyfingers can be bought at most supermarkets or bakeries.

19

Strawberry Whip

Here's what you need:

1 package (10 ounces) frozen sliced strawberries, beginning to thaw
1 package ladyfingers
1 cup whipped cream (page 22)
can opener
strainer
medium-size bowl
regular tablespoon or mixing spoon
4 custard cups

YOU MAY NEED HELP OPENING THE FROZEN STRAWBERRIES

Here's what you do:

1. Place strainer over bowl. Pour strawberries into strainer to drain liquid.
2. Tear ladyfingers (or cut with table knife) in half the long way. Line bottoms and sides of custard cups to make pastry cups.
3. Add drained strawberries to whipped cream. Stir gently. Spoon into cups.
4. Chill in refrigerator for 1 hour or more.

Makes 4 servings

Note: You may use other drained fruits or sliced bananas.
Ladyfingers can be bought at most supermarkets and bakeries.

Whipped Cream

Here's what you need:

1 small container (1 cup) heavy cream chilled	narrow deep bowl
2 tablespoons sugar	egg beater
1 teaspoon vanilla extract	measuring spoons

Here's what you do:

1. If the weather is warm, chill bowl and egg beater.
2. Pour cream into bowl.
3. Beat until cream begins to thicken but can still be turned easily.
4. Dip 1-tablespoon measuring spoon into sugar. Sprinkle over cream. Dip again and sprinkle.
5. Beat again.
6. Pour vanilla into 1-teaspoon measuring spoon held over cup. (Cup catches any spills.) Add to cream.
7. Beat until stiff, but do not overbeat or cream turns to butter.

Makes 2 cups whipped cream

Note: To make 1 cup of whipped cream, measure ½ cup heavy cream into bowl. Follow directions above adding 1 tablespoon sugar and ½ teaspoon vanilla extract.

Leftover whipped cream may be stored in a covered container in the refrigerator or freezer.

Banana Shake

Here's what you need:

1 small ripe banana
⅔ cup half-and-half cream or
   milk
1 teaspoon almond flavoring
fork
medium-size bowl

1-cup measuring cup
measuring spoons
regular cup
egg beater
1 tall glass for serving

Here's what you do:

1. Peel banana. Mash with fork in bowl.
2. Pour cream or milk into 1-cup measuring cup up to ⅔ line. Add to banana.
3. Pour almond flavoring into 1-teaspoon measuring spoon held over cup. (If you spill, the cup catches the overflow.) Add measured almond flavoring.
4. Beat with egg beater until thoroughly mixed and frothy.
5. Pour into tall glass.

                                        Makes 1 serving

Eggnog

Here's what you need:

1 egg	egg beater
2 teaspoons sugar	measuring spoons
1 cup milk	1-cup measuring cup
1 teaspoon vanilla extract	regular cup
½ teaspoon nutmeg	1 tall glass for serving
small narrow bowl	

Here's what you do:

1. Break egg into bowl.
2. Beat egg with beater until you count to eight or ten.
3. Dip 1-teaspoon measuring spoon into sugar. Add to egg. Dip again and add sugar to egg.
4. Pour milk into 1-cup measuring cup up to top line.
5. Pour vanilla into 1-teaspoon measuring spoon held over regular cup. (If you spill, the cup catches the overflow.) Add vanilla to bowl.
6. Dip ½-teaspoon measuring spoon into nutmeg. Sprinkle over bowl.
7. Beat mixture again until you count to eight or ten.
8. Pour into tall glass.

Makes 1 serving

Fruit Milk Shake

Here's what you need:

1⅓ cups cold fruit juice (apricot, raspberry, pear, whatever you choose)

2⅓ cups cold half-and-half cream or milk

1 teaspoon cinnamon

can opener

4-cup measuring cup

quart jar with lid

measuring spoons

4 tall glasses for serving

LET AN ADULT OPEN THE FRUIT JUICE

Here's what you do:

1. Pour fruit juice into 4-cup measuring cup up to the 1⅓-cup line. Pour into quart jar.
2. Pour cream into the same 4-cup measuring cup up to the 2⅓-cup line. Add to juice.
3. Dip 1-teaspoon measuring spoon into cinnamon. Sprinkle cinnamon over juice and milk mixture.
4. Fasten lid so that it stays tight. Shake jar about five times, and count as you do it.
5. Pour into tall glasses.

Makes 4 servings

Peanut Butter Frosted

Here's what you need:

½ pint vanilla ice cream   mixing bowl
¼ cup smooth peanut butter   tablespoon
1 cup cold milk   egg beater
1 ripe medium-size banana   table fork
table knife   2 tall glasses for serving
nested measuring cups

Here's what you do:

1. Remove ice cream from freezer to soften.
2. Use table knife to scoop peanut butter out of jar and into ¼ nested cup. Empty peanut butter into bowl.
3. Pour milk into 1-cup measuring cup up to top line. Add half of it to peanut butter. Beat with egg beater.
4. Add remaining milk. Beat with egg beater until mixed.
5. Peel and mash banana with table fork. Add to bowl. Beat with egg beater.
6. Add ice cream and beat until thoroughly mixed.
7. Pour into tall glasses.

Note: A milk shake is a "frosted" when ice cream and other ingredients are mixed thoroughly.

Lemonade

Here's what you need:

1 lemon   small bowl
2 to 3 tablespoons sugar   measuring spoons
1¼ cups water   2-cup measuring cup
2 ice cubes   regular tablespoon
paring knife for the adult to use   2 glasses for serving
lemon squeezer

ASK AN ADULT TO CUT THE LEMON IN HALF

Here's what you do:

1. Place lemon squeezer on bowl. Press 1 half of lemon on squeezer until all juice is squeezed. Press second half of lemon and squeeze.
2. Dip 1-tablespoon measuring spoon into sugar. Add to lemon juice. Dip again and add to juice.
3. Run water from faucet into 2-cup measuring cup until 1¼-cup line is reached. Mix with lemon juice. Stir with regular tablespoon to melt sugar.
4. Taste to see if more sugar is needed for your taste.

Blackberry Patch Salad

Here's what you need:

1 can (1 pound, 13 ounces) pears
lettuce leaves
1 small container (4 ounces)
  whipped cream cheese
about 12 blackberries, fresh,
  frozen, or canned

¼ cup shelled sunflower seeds
can opener
salad plates
table fork
table knife

ASK AN ADULT TO OPEN CANS AND THROW AWAY TOPS

Here's what you do:

1. Place lettuce leaves on 3 plates.
2. With fork, place 2 pear halves on lettuce, cut side down. Pat dry with paper towel.
3. Spread cream cheese over pear halves.
4. Decorate each pear half with several drained blackberries.
5. Sprinkle with sunflower seeds.

Makes 3 servings

34

5. Add 1 or 2 ice cubes.
6. Pour into glasses.

Makes 2 medium servings

Note: 1 lemon makes about 3 tablespoons of juice.

31

Tomato and Cucumber Juice

Here's what you need:

1 cucumber	table knife
2 cups tomato juice	wooden cutting board
1 tablespoon vegetable oil	quart jar with lid
½ teaspoon salt	2-cup measuring cup
pepper	measuring spoons
4 ice cubes	regular cup
vegetable peeler	4 glasses for serving

YOU MAY NEED GROWN-UP HELP TO CHOP THE CUCUMBER FINE ENOUGH

Here's what you do:

1. Wash and dry cucumber. Peel with vegetable peeler.
2. Chop fine with table knife on wooden cutting board. Put chopped cucumber in quart jar.
3. Pour tomato juice into 2-cup measuring cup up to the top line. Add to cucumber in jar.
4. Pour oil into 1-tablespoon measuring spoon held over cup. (If you spill, cup catches the overflow.) Add to jar.
5. Pour salt into ½-teaspoon measuring spoon held over cup. Add to jar along with sprinkle of pepper.
6. Add 4 ice cubes.
7. Fasten lid so that it stays tight. Shake jar about five times. Count as you do it.
8. Pour into glasses.

Makes 4 servings

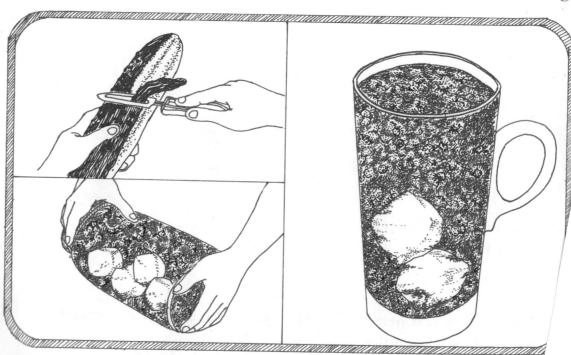

Chicken Salad

Here's what you need:

1 small can (5 ounces) canned   table knife
    chicken, or ½ cup leftover   wooden cutting board
    cooked chicken   mixing bowl
4 or 5 inner stalks celery   1-cup measuring cup
small amount of mayonnaise   regular tablespoon
salt and pepper to taste   mixing spoon
lettuce leaves   platter or large plate for serving
can opener

ASK AN ADULT TO OPEN CAN AND THROW AWAY TOP

Here's what you do:

1. Cut chicken on wooden board in small pieces with table knife. Put in mixing bowl.
2. Wash and dry celery. Cut into small pieces. Add to chicken.
3. Add a small amount of mayonnaise, about 2 regular tablespoons, depending upon how moist the chicken is.
4. Add salt and pepper. Mix thoroughly.

5. Place several crisp lettuce leaves on platter. Heap chicken salad in center.
6. If you have sliced pickles or olives in the refrigerator place them around the chicken.

Makes 2 small servings

5. Add 1 or 2 ice cubes.
6. Pour into glasses.

Makes 2 medium servings

Note: 1 lemon makes about 3 tablespoons of juice.

Tomato and Cucumber Juice

Here's what you need:

1 cucumber	table knife
2 cups tomato juice	wooden cutting board
1 tablespoon vegetable oil	quart jar with lid
½ teaspoon salt	2-cup measuring cup
pepper	measuring spoons
4 ice cubes	regular cup
vegetable peeler	4 glasses for serving

YOU MAY NEED GROWN-UP HELP TO CHOP THE CUCUMBER FINE ENOUGH

Here's what you do:

1. Wash and dry cucumber. Peel with vegetable peeler.
2. Chop fine with table knife on wooden cutting board. Put chopped cucumber in quart jar.
3. Pour tomato juice into 2-cup measuring cup up to the top line. Add to cucumber in jar.
4. Pour oil into 1-tablespoon measuring spoon held over cup. (If you spill, cup catches the overflow.) Add to jar.

5. Pour salt into ½-teaspoon measuring spoon held over cup. Add to jar along with sprinkle of pepper.
6. Add 4 ice cubes.
7. Fasten lid so that it stays tight. Shake jar about five times. Count as you do it.
8. Pour into glasses.   **Makes 4 servings**

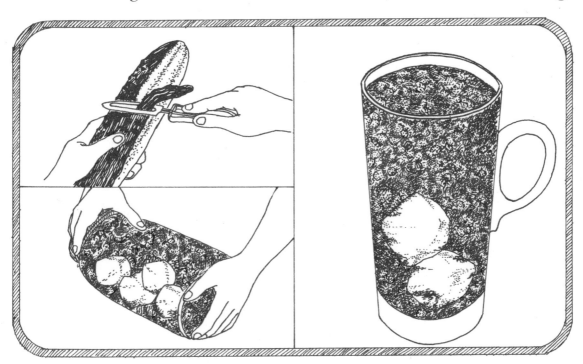

Blackberry Patch Salad

Here's what you need:

1 can (1 pound, 13 ounces) pears
lettuce leaves
1 small container (4 ounces)
   whipped cream cheese
about 12 blackberries, fresh,
   frozen, or canned

¼ cup shelled sunflower seeds
can opener
salad plates
table fork
table knife

ASK AN ADULT TO OPEN CANS AND THROW AWAY TOPS

Here's what you do:

1. Place lettuce leaves on 3 plates.
2. With fork, place 2 pear halves on lettuce, cut side down. Pat dry with paper towel.
3. Spread cream cheese over pear halves.
4. Decorate each pear half with several drained blackberries.
5. Sprinkle with sunflower seeds.

Makes 3 servings

Cold Meat Salad

Here's what you need:

about 6 to 8 slices cooked meat (ham, pork, beef), enough to make 2 cups chopped meat
3 or 4 inner stalks celery
2 tablespoons pickle relish
salt and pepper to taste
French salad dressing
lettuce leaves

wooden cutting board
table knife
2-cup measuring cup
mixing bowl
measuring spoons
salad bowl for serving
wooden mixing spoon

Here's what you do:

1. On cutting board, cut cooked meat into small pieces, about ½ inch. Place in measuring cup up to 2-cup line. Put in mixing bowl.
2. Wash and dry celery. Cut into small pieces. Add to meat.

3. Dip 1-tablespoon measuring spoon in pickle relish and add to meat. Measure second tablespoon. Add to meat.
4. Sprinkle lightly with salt and pepper.
5. Pour 3 to 4 tablespoons French salad dressing over meat and mix.
6. Place lettuce leaves around salad bowl. Spoon salad into it.

Makes 4 to 6 servings

Cucumber Nut Salad

Here's what you need:

2 cucumbers
salt and pepper
1 container (1 cup) dairy sour
   cream
¼ cup shelled sunflower seeds
vegetable brush
vegetable peeler

table knife
wooden cutting board
mixing bowl
fork
¼-cup nested measuring cup
regular tablespoon
4 small salad bowls

Here's what you do:

1. Scrub cucumbers with vegetable brush under running water. Dry with paper towel. If skin is tough, peel with vegetable peeler.
2. Slice with table knife, very thin.

3. Put in bowl. Sprinkle with salt and pepper. Mix with fork.
4. Pour shelled sunflower seeds into ¼ cup measuring cup. Sprinkle over cucumbers.
5. Spoon sour cream over cucumbers. Mix carefully.
6. Cover with transparent plastic wrap. Place in refrigerator to chill for at least 1 hour.
7. Serve in 4 small salad bowls.

Makes 4 servings

Macaroni Salad

Here's what you need:

2 cups cooked macaroni	table knife
3 or 4 inner stalks celery	wooden cutting board
1 small bunch parsley	scissors
½ cup mayonnaise	½-cup nested measuring cup
onion salt and pepper	mixing spoon
lettuce leaves	platter or shallow bowl for serving
mixing bowl	

ASK AN ADULT TO COOK AND DRAIN MACARONI

Here's what you do:

1. Put cooled macaroni in mixing bowl.
2. Wash and dry celery stalks. Cut into small pieces on wooden cutting board. Add to macaroni.
3. Wash and dry parsley. Cut with scissors. Add to macaroni.

4. Spoon mayonnaise into ½-cup measuring cup and into macaroni.
5. Sprinkle with onion salt and pepper. Mix with spoon.
6. Line platter or bowl with lettuce leaves. Place macaroni salad in center.
7. Cover with transparent plastic wrap.
8. Put in refrigerator for 2 or 3 hours until chilled.
9. Remove wrap from bowl and serve.

Makes 4 to 6 servings

Suggestions for Making Sandwiches

Here's what you need:

Bread or rolls
   white, whole wheat, rye
   canned breads like brown
     bread and date-nut
Butter or margarine

Filling of your choice:
   meat, chicken, turkey, cheese,
     vegetables, peanut butter,
     sliced egg

Here's what you do:

1. To soften butter or margarine:
   Take out of refrigerator about 30 minutes before sandwich making,
   or . . .
   Place in bowl. Mash with back of wooden spoon. Beat until smooth,
   or . . .
   Buy whipped butter or margarine.
2. Choose the filling you like. Place by cutting board.
3. Place bread nearby. Take 2 slices of bread and place on cutting board.

4. Spread butter lightly on one side of bread. Spread the other slice with mayonnaise, mustard, or butter, depending upon the filling.
5. Place filling on 1 slice. Top with the other slice.
6. Sandwiches with soft fillings can be cut with a table knife. Those with meat may have to be cut by an adult.
7. If you are not eating immediately, cover sandwich completely with transparent plastic wrap and place in refrigerator.

Apple-Peanut Butter Sandwiches

Here's what you need:

4 slices of bread
butter or margarine, softened
1 apple
½ cup peanut butter
grater
small bowl

vegetable peeler
½-cup nested measuring cup
table knife
table fork
wooden cutting board

Here's what you do:

1. Follow suggestions on page 43-44.
2. Place grater over small bowl.
3. Wash and dry 1 small apple. Remove stem and core with vegetable peeler. Leave apple whole to make grating easier. Grate carefully.
4. Fill ½-cup measuring cup with peanut butter. (A table knife is easier to use than a spoon.) Add to apple. Mix thoroughly.
5. Spread filling on bread. Top with bread.

Makes enough for 3 or 4 sandwiches

Cucumber and Cream Cheese Sandwiches

Here's what you need:

1 medium cucumber	salt and pepper
4 slices cracked wheat or white bread	vegetable brush
	vegetable peeler
1 small container (4 ounces) whipped cream cheese	table knife
	wooden chopping board

Here's what you do:

1. Scrub cucumbers under running water with brush, dry and peel.
2. Spread one side of each slice of bread lightly with cream cheese.
3. Slice cucumbers very thin with table knife. Place on bread.
4. Sprinkle with salt and pepper. Top with bread.

Makes 2 servings

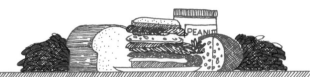

Date and Nut Sandwiches

Here's what you need:

1 can (10 ounces) brown bread
butter or margarine
1 cup chopped dates (read label
   to choose correctly)
2 tablespoons shelled sunflower
   seeds
1 small container (4 ounces)
   whipped cream cheese

can opener
wooden cutting board
1-cup measuring cup
small mixing bowl
measuring spoons
mixing spoon
table knife

ASK A GROWNUP TO OPEN CAN AND THROW AWAY THE TOP

Here's what you do:

1. Follow suggestions on page 43-44.
2. Spoon dates into measuring cup up to 1-cup line. Empty into bowl.

3. Dip 1-tablespoon measuring spoon into package of sunflower seeds. Sprinkle over dates. Dip spoon again and sprinkle over dates.
4. Spoon whipped cream cheese into bowl. Mix thoroughly.
5. Slice bread with table knife.
6. Spread date mixture on bread. Top with slices.

¼ can brown bread and this spread
make about 8 thin sandwiches

Meat and Cheese Sandwiches

Here's what you need:

4 slices bread
butter, softened
mustard
2 slices meat, like bologna or
   boiled ham

2 slices American cheese
2 lettuce leaves
table knife
table fork
wooden cutting board

Here's what you do:

1.   Follow sandwich suggestions page 43-44.
2.   Place a slice of bologna or boiled ham on 2 slices of bread.
3.   Top with mustard, slice of cheese, lettuce leaf and bread.
4.   If cheese is too wide, cut with table knife and use for next sandwich.

4 slices of bread make 2 servings

Peanut Butter in Seven Ways

Here's what you need:

2 slices bread
butter or margarine
peanut butter
any of the following: bacon, small
  banana, dill pickle, pickle

relish, cream cheese, honey, or
  jelly
wooden cutting board
table knife
teaspoon

Here's what you do:

1. Follow sandwich suggestions on page 43-44.
2. Spread peanut butter on buttered bread. Add 2 or 3 slices of crisp bacon. Top with remaining bread.

      -or-

3. Spread peanut butter on buttered bread. Slice 1 banana and add. Top with bread.

-or-

4. Spread peanut butter on buttered bread. Slice dill pickle very thin and add. Top with bread.

    -or-

5. Spread peanut butter on buttered bread. Spoon pickle relish without juice over peanut butter. Top with bread.

    -or-

6. Spread peanut butter on buttered bread. Spread cream cheese over peanut butter. Top with bread.

    -or-

7. Spread peanut butter on buttered bread. Spoon honey over peanut butter. Top with bread.

    -or-

8. Spread peanut butter on buttered bread. Spread jelly over peanut butter. Top with bread.

2 slices make 1 serving.

Sandwich Circles

Cut 2 circles from thin slices of bread with doughnut or round cookie cutter. Spread circle with filling and top with other circle.

Funny Faces

Cut circle. Spread bread with cream cheese or peanut butter. Use raisins for eyes, nose, and mouth.

Sandwich Boats

Take bread from center of soft roll. Fill with favorite sandwich spread. Use a sprig of parsley for a sail.

Apple Snack

Here's what you need:

1 apple	table knife
1 small can (6 ounces) pineapple juice or leftover juice from canned pineapple	wooden cutting board
	small bowl
peanut butter	table fork
can opener	small plate

LET AN ADULT OPEN CAN AND THROW AWAY TOP

Here's what you do:

1. Wash and dry apple. Slice into thin slices. Place slices in bowl.
2. Cover with pineapple juice for 15 to 30 minutes.
3. Remove slices from juice with fork. Spread with peanut butter.
4. Serve on small plate.

Makes 1 or 2 servings

Arabian Dates

Here's what you need:

1 small bar (4 ounces) cream
   cheese
1 tablespoon wheat germ
1 tablespoon honey
1 package (8 ounces) pitted dates

small bowl
table fork
measuring spoons
table knife
wax paper

Here's what you do:

1. Mash cream cheese in small bowl with fork.
2. Dip 1-tablespoon measuring spoon into jar of wheat germ. Sprinkle over cream cheese.
3. Dip same 1-tablespoon measuring spoon into jar of honey. Add to bowl.
4. Mix thoroughly.
5. Stuff dates with cream cheese mixture using table knife. Place on wax paper. Chill in refrigerator.

Makes about 38 stuffed dates

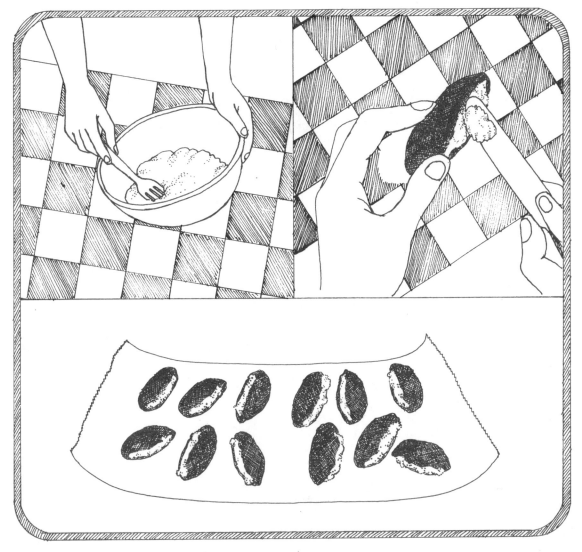

Maple-Flavored Snack

Here's what you need:

⅓ cup peanut butter　　　　　1-cup measuring cup
⅓ cup maple-flavored sirup　　table fork
crackers　　　　　　　　　　table knife

Here's what you do:

1. Put peanut butter into measuring cup up to ⅓ cup line.
2. Into that same cup, pour maple-flavored sirup up to ⅔ line.
3. Mix slowly but thoroughly with fork.
4. Spread on crackers.

Spreads about 12 large crackers

Vegetable Snacks

Here's what you need:

carrots
cauliflower
inner celery stalks
small jar processed cheese spread
salt and pepper

vegetable brush
vegetable parer
large bowl with ice
wooden cutting board
table knife

LET AN ADULT HELP WITH CUTTING OFF TOPS OF CARROTS AND REMOVING OUTSIDE LEAVES FROM CAULIFLOWER.

Here's what you do:

To make carrot curls

1. Scrub carrots under cool running water with brush.
2. With vegetable parer, slowly make a long strip from top to bottom of carrot.

3. Curl strip around finger. Carefully remove carrot strip and place in ice water. Continue making strips.

 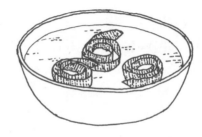

For cauliflower

1. Wash under cool running water.
2. Break head into small flowerets.
3. Place in ice water to chill.

For stuffed celery

1. Wash and dry inner celery stalks.
2. With table knife, fill stalks with cheese.

Take carrot curls and cauliflower from water. Pat them dry. Place on large platter or relish dish with stuffed celery. Salt and pepper vegetables. Serve immediately.

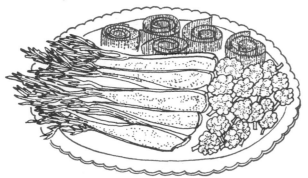

Apricot Candy

Here's what you need:

1 cup dried apricots

⅓ cup nonfat dry milk powder

1 cup packaged flaked coconut

¼ cup maple-flavored sirup

1 tablespoon butter or
 margarine, softened

about ½ cup wheat germ

1-cup measuring cup

kitchen scissors

mixing bowl

measuring spoons

wax paper

Here's what you do:

1. Measure apricots in measuring cup to 1-cup line. Cut apricots into small pieces with kitchen scissors. Put in bowl.
2. Pour dry milk powder into measuring cup up to ⅓-cup line. Add to apricots.
3. Spoon coconut into measuring cup up to 1-cup line. Mix with dry milk and apricots.
4. Pour maple-flavored sirup into measuring cup to ¼-cup line. Add to bowl.
5. Measure butter with 1-tablespoon measuring spoon. Add to mixture.
6. Stir everything together with mixing spoon or hands.

7. Form mixture into small balls about the size of a walnut.
8. Pour wheat germ on piece of wax paper and roll balls in it.
9. Cover with another piece of wax paper. Place in refrigerator for several hours to chill.

Makes 20 candies

Fondant Candy

Here's what you need:

⅓ cup butter, softened	⅓-cup nested measuring cup
⅓ cup white corn sirup	mixing bowl
½ teaspoon salt	measuring spoons
1 teaspoon vanilla extract	regular cup
1-pound box confectioners' sugar	mixing spoon
⅓ cup wheat germ	wax paper

Here's what you do:

1. Place softened butter in measuring cup. Spoon into mixing bowl.
2. Pour sirup into same measuring cup (it is not necessary to wash cup). Add to butter.
3. Pour salt into ½-teaspoon measuring spoon held over regular cup. (Cup will catch overflow.) Sprinkle over butter.
4. Pour vanilla into 1-teaspoon measuring spoon over cup. Add to butter.
5. Mix thoroughly.
6. Slowly add sugar, mixing all the time.

7. Pour wheat germ into washed and dried measuring cup. Stir into mixture.
8. Form ball of fondant candy on piece of wax paper. Press flat with palm of hand. Repeat this motion, which is called "kneading."
9. Smooth candy evenly on wax paper with hands. Cut into squares or other shapes.
10. Cover with wax paper. Place in refrigerator to chill.

Makes about 1 ½ pounds of candy

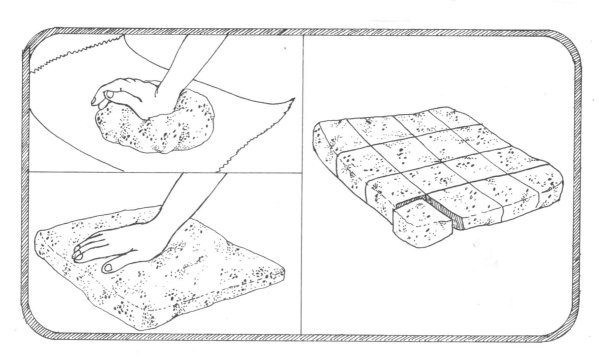

ABOUT THE AUTHOR: Aileen Paul has taught Saturday morning cooking classes for girls and boys for eleven years and continues to do so despite a busy professional life as an award-winning broadcaster, writer, and television food specialist. Aileen Paul has found a way of writing for children that is clear and simple yet contains a special ingredient—encouragement. She says, "Children do best when they are encouraged to make decisions that are appropriate for their age, and to follow through with those decisions and the successes or failures that result. Joyful activities like cooking, gardening, and camping offer such opportunities."

Aileen Paul is author, in collaboration with artist Arthur Hawkins, of KIDS COOKING and CANDIES, COOKIES, CAKES, and author of KIDS GARDENING, KIDS CAMPING, and KIDS COOKING COMPLETE MEALS.

ABOUT THE ILLUSTRATOR: Carol Inouye was born in California and spent her early childhood in the Far East. She returned to the United States when she was ten years old. Ms. Inouye attended the University of California at Los Angeles and Chouinard Art Institute. She has worked as a graphic designer and as art director for publishing houses and is currently free-lancing as an illustrator and graphic designer. NATURECRAFT, written and illustrated by Ms. Inouye, is her first book for children. She is presently a resident of New York City.